Machines at Work

Machines on a Construction Site

Siân Smith

Raintree

Raintree is an imprint of Capstone Global Library Limited, a company incorporated in England and Wales having its registered office at 7 Pilgrim Street, London, EC4V 6LB – Registered company number: 6695582

www.raintreepublishers.co.uk
myorders@raintreepublishers.co.uk

Text © Capstone Global Library Limited 2014
First published in hardback in 2014
Paperback edition first published in 2015
The moral rights of the proprietor have been asserted.

Edited by Dan Nunn and John-Paul Wilkins
Designed by Cynthia Akiyoshi
Picture research by Elizabeth Alexander
Production by Helen McCreath
Originated by Capstone Global Library Ltd
Printed and bound in China by Leo Paper Products Ltd

ISBN 978 1 406 25937 7 (hardback)
17 16 15 14 13
10 9 8 7 6 5 4 3 2 1

ISBN 978 1 406 25942 1 (paperback)
18 17 16 15 14
10 9 8 7 6 5 4 3 2 1

British Library Cataloguing in Publication Data
Smith, Siân.
Machines on a construction site. – (Machines at work)
690'.028-dc23
A full catalogue record for this book is available from the British Library.

Acknowledgements
We would like to thank the following for permission to reproduce photographs: Alamy pp. 7 (© Robert Convery), 8 (© G P Bowater), 16 (© paul ridsdale), 19 (© Everyday Images), 23 grapple (© PhotoAlto); Getty Images pp. title page (narvikk/Vetta), 14 (Creti Stefano/Flickr); Shutterstock pp. 4, 23 construction site (© Yuriy Chertok), 5, 11, 23 excavator (© Dmitry Kalinovsky), 9, 23 tracks (© Norman Bateman), 10 (© Toa55), 12 (© AlexKZ), 13, 23 dump box (© Johan Larson), 18 (© David Hughes), 21 (© Rigucci), 22 (© marilyn barbone); SuperStock pp. 6 (© Richard Heinzen/Purestock), 15, 23 cab (© Science Faction), 17 (© Reino Hannine/age footstock), 20 (© Tetra Images).

Design element photographs of car engine part (© fuyu liu), crane (© Nolte Lourens), gear cog (© Leremy), and tyre tread (© Robert J. Beyers II) reproduced with permission of Shutterstock.

Front cover photograph of excavator on construction site reproduced with permission of Getty Images (narvikk/Vetta). Back cover photographs of calfdozer (© Norman Bateman) and dumper truck (© Johan Larson) reproduced with permission of Shutterstock.

We would like to thank Dee Reid and Marla Conn for their invaluable help in the preparation of this book.

Contents

Some words are shown in bold, **like this**. You can find out what they mean by looking in the glossary.

Why are there machines on a construction site?

A **construction site** is a place where things are built.

Builders could be making bridges, roads, houses, or other buildings.

There are many different jobs that need to be done on a construction site.

Machines make the jobs safer and easier to do.

Which machines help to smash things up?

Sometimes buildings have to be knocked down before new ones can be built.

Cranes swing heavy wrecking balls to knock buildings down.

crane

wrecking ball

drill

concrete

Sometimes construction workers need to break up the ground.

Powerful drills are used to break up hard concrete.

Which machines get the ground ready for building?

A bulldozer has a large blade at the front. This is used to clear the ground.

Most bulldozers have **tracks** instead of wheels. This helps them to move on lumpy ground and mud.

blade

track

calf dozer

Small bulldozers are called calf dozers.
They are useful because they can get
into small spaces.

A machine called a grader makes the ground smooth and ready to build on.

The long blade scrapes along the ground to make it flat.

blade

bucket

Wheel loaders are used to scoop up soil or rocks and carry them away.

The bucket at the front moves down to shovel things in, then lifts up to carry them.

11

Which machines carry rocks, soil, and sand?

Wheel loaders often move rocks, soil, and sand into dumper trucks.

Dumper trucks are big and powerful enough to carry huge loads.

wheel loader

dumper truck

dump box

The container or **dump box** can be lifted up so that the load tips out easily.

Most dumper trucks tip out their loads at the back, but some tip at the sides.

13

What are digger machines used for?

Diggers are very useful machines for building work. They are also called backhoes or **excavators**.

The bucket can be used for many things such as digging, loading, or carrying.

bucket

arm

cab

The bottom part of a digger holds it steady. The driver's **cab** and digging arm can move around in a circle.

The long arm on a digger means it can reach high and far, and dig down deep.

Can diggers do other jobs?

The bucket on a digger can be swapped for other tools.

Magnets, or giant claws called **grapples,** can be put on a digger to lift things up.

magnet

rock breaker

Other tools such as saws, hammers, and rock breakers can be put on a digger to break things up.

Drills can be put on a digger to make holes in the ground.

What is a backhoe loader?

A backhoe loader is actually two different machines made into one.

The front of the machine is a wheel loader and the back is a digger. Can you tell which is which?

cab

The seat inside the **cab** turns round so that the driver can use both machines.

Backhoe loaders are used to do a lot of work on **construction sites**.

Which machines are used to reach high places?

Buildings on a **construction site** can be very tall.

Machines with moving platforms called cherry pickers can lift builders up high.

tower crane

Cranes are used to move heavy materials up and down.

Cranes can be fixed to the ground or to lorries. Some cranes can be made taller to match the height of a building.

What does this machine do?

Can you guess what this **construction site** machine does?

Find the answer on page 24.